SELF-DEFENCE
for Women

by Captain W. E. Fairbairn
*Late Assistant Commissioner
Shanghai Municipal Police*

with photographs by
F. A. R. Leitao
Late Major, Shanghai Volunteer Corps

Copyright © 2011 Read Books Ltd.
This book is copyright and may not be
reproduced or copied in any way without
the express permission of the publisher in writing

British Library Cataloguing-in-Publication Data
A catalogue record for this book is available from
the British Library

NOTE.—It should be noted that the author lived in Shanghai from 1907 until quite recently. For years he was the Instructor in Self-Defence to the Shanghai Municipal Police and includes, among his other pupils, royalty and several of the highest Jiu-jitsu experts of Japan. He has made a scientific study of practically every known method of self-defence, including the following:

Japanese Jiu-jitsu: For which he holds the Second Degree Black Belt of Kodokan Jiu-jitsu University, Tokyo, Japan. The author is the first foreigner living outside of Japan to be awarded a Black Belt Degree by Kodokan Jiu-jitsu University.

Chinese 'boxing': Studied under Tsai Ching Tung, who at one time was employed at the Imperial Palace, Peking, as an Instructor to Retainers of the late Dowager Empress.

FOREWORD

This book is based upon an earlier work issued under the name of *Défendu*, which was written in 1925 for the police forces of the Far East. Later a second edition of *Défendu* was printed to meet the demand for copies from police and physical directors all over the world. In 1931 the demand for copies from the United States of America was met by another edition under the title of *Scientific Self-Defence*, published by D. Appleton & Company, New York. A revised and much enlarged edition of this book is published in this country under the title, *All-in Fighting*.

The methods of defence in these books were for men who in their everyday walk of life had to frequent places where they were liable to be attacked, and the methods employed to deal with these attacks were admittedly drastic and unpleasant, but were all justifiable and necessary to self protection against the foul methods that are used by a certain class. The fact that not one of these methods has had to be changed, on account of being impracticable, or for any other reason, is very gratifying and it is partly owing to this and the many requests of friends that this book, SELF-DEFENCE FOR WOMEN AND GIRLS, is being published.

The author, in his early days as a member of the Legation Guard in Seoul, was first initiated into the scientific method of fighting with the butt-end of the rifle and can well remember the shock he received when he found that a method of attack, which at that time, 1904–5, was unheard of, was being used against him. The team of which he was a member had previously carried everything before them, but they met their Waterloo, being all badly beaten by opponents practically half their size. When the shock to their dignity had worn off and they had time to study carefully the methods employed by the opposing team, they were unanimous that only the surprise of the unexpected method used had been the cause of their defeat. This was clearly proved at a later date. The author has never forgotten the lesson taught him that day: provided that you take the fight to your opponent's camp and apply original and unexpected methods of attack, seventy-five per cent of the battle is won.

It is this 'surprise' and the unexpectedness of attack that the

FOREWORD

author mainly depends upon in applying the methods illustrated in this book, and students can rest assured that they will also find it useful.

There are many persons with an erroneous impression concerning the Art of Jiu-jitsu. Quite a number of them are under the impression that it is only necessary to take one or two lessons, after which they will be able to throw their opponents over their heads. There are others who believe that immediately a Jiu-jitsu expert catches hold of his opponent he will, by some secret Oriental method, throw him and break his arm or leg or render him unconscious. The reason for this being so generally believed is partly the fact that any two persons, without the slightest knowledge of any method of wrestling, could with a few rehearsals stage a demonstration that would easily deceive those not acquainted with the art, and partly the present day public demand for the spectacular.

Weight and strength, either in attack or defence, must always be an advantage and an asset to those possessing them. Unless you are prepared to spend years in the study of the art of falling and of how to use your opponent's weight and strength to your advantage, you can rest assured that you will never throw your opponent over your head—UNLESS HE IS WILLING THAT YOU SHOULD DO SO.

Every method of defence explained and illustrated in this book has been specially selected for girls and they are all practicable. It will be noted that they do not call for more strength than that possessed by the average girl of seventeen. Many of the methods are original and worked-out by the author in answer to: 'What would you do, if you were held like this?'

Students who wish to go more deeply into the study of this Art are referred to my other book, *All-in Fighting*.

NOTE:—For the purpose of uniformity all illustrations are shown for the right hand, but they can, of course, be equally well applied with the left.

W. E. FAIRBAIRN

CONTENTS

	Foreword	*page* 5
No. 1	Wrist Hold (One Hand)	8
No. 2	Wrist Hold (Two Hands)	9
No. 3	Being Strangled (One Hand)	11
No. 4	How to Apply the "Chin Jab"	13
No. 5	Being Strangled (Two Hands)	15
No. 6	"Bear Hug"—From in Front	16
No. 7	"Bear Hug"—From Behind	17
No. 8	Waist Hold—From in Front	19
No. 9	Waist Hold—From Behind	21
No. 10	Hair Hold—From Behind	23
No. 11	Coat Hold	25
No. 12	Coat Hold	27
No. 13	Belt Hold	29
No. 14	Simple Counters	31
No. 15	Umbrella Drill	33
No. 16	Being Held from in Front	35
No. 17	The "Cinema" Hold	39
No. 18	Matchbox (Warning)	43
No. 19	Car "Hold-Up"	45
No. 20	"Give Me a Light"	47
	Conclusion	48

DEFENCE AGAINST VARIOUS HOLDS

No. I. Wrist Hold (One Hand)

Your assailant seizes your right wrist with his left hand, Fig. 1. To make him release his hold: bend your arm from the elbow, upwards and towards your body, then twist your wrist towards and over his thumb, Fig. 2.

Note: The above must be one continuous movement and carried out with speed.

Fig. 1   Fig. 2

DEFENCE AGAINST VARIOUS HOLDS

No. 2. Wrist Hold (Two Hands)

Your assailant seizes you by both wrists, Fig. 3. To make him release his hold: bend your arms towards your body and twist your wrists in the direction of his thumbs.

Or: jerk your hands towards your body, at the same time hitting him in the face with the top of your head, Fig. 4.

Fig. 3   Fig. 4

DEFENCE AGAINST VARIOUS HOLDS

No. 3. Being Strangled (One Hand)

Fig. 5   Fig. 6

DEFENCE AGAINST VARIOUS HOLDS

No. 3. Being Strangled (One Hand)

Your assailant seizes you by the throat with his right hand, forcing you back against a wall, Fig. 5.

1. With a sharp blow of your right hand strike his right wrist towards your left-hand side.
2. If necessary, knee him in the pit of the stomach with your right knee, Fig. 6.

Note: The position demonstrated in Fig. 5 (Forced back against a wall) was selected because it shows the only position where it would be possible, by means of a Strangle Hold, for an assailant to do you any harm. In the event of anyone attempting to strangle you with only one hand and you are clear of a wall or other obstruction, all that is necessary to break the hold, is to suddenly step backwards or sideways in the direction of his thumb.

If we were asked to give a demonstration of defence against this One-Hand Strangle Hold, we would select the position shown in Fig. 5—Against a Wall. Further, if our opponent puts all his strength and weight into the hold, the better it would suit us—a sharp blow as in Fig. 6, with the palm of the right hand on the thumb-side of his wrist, is all that is necessary to make him release his hold.

DEFENCE AGAINST VARIOUS HOLDS

No. 4. How to Apply the "Chin Jab"

Fig. 7

Fig. 8

Fig. 9

DEFENCE AGAINST VARIOUS HOLDS

No. 4. How to Apply the "Chin Jab"

In Defence Holds No. 5, Being Strangled (Two Hands), No. 8, Waist Hold From the Front, and No. 10, Hair Hold (From Behind), it will be noted one of the methods to deal with your assailant is referred to as a "Chin Jab". This blow is struck with the base or heel of the palm of the hand at the "Point of the Chin" and if applied correctly is liable to render your assailant unconscious.

CAUTION: The "Chin Jab" must only be used where the circumstances fully justify such drastic methods being applied and students are advised to put in their practice at "Shadow Drill", not on their friends.

1. Bend the right arm from the elbow, turning the palm of the hand to the front, Fig. 7.

2. Bend the palm of the hand backwards as far as possible, extending the fingers and thumb, and keep them bent (Fig. 8) so that, in the event of your missing your assailant's chin, they will reach his eyes, should the situation justify such drastic action.

Note: The force of this blow does not depend upon the strength of the person applying it, but upon keeping the palm of the hand bent backwards. This permits one to deliver a "rock-crushing" blow with a follow-through from the shoulder and no possibility of hurting one's own hand when applying it.

3. The position of the hand in Fig. 8 was selected as the best to demonstrate the relative position of the fingers, thumb, and palm of the hand. Students will find that a position somewhat as in Fig. 9 will be a more practical position from which to start this blow.

DEFENCE AGAINST VARIOUS HOLDS

No. 5. Being Strangled (Two Hands)

Fig. 10

DEFENCE AGAINST VARIOUS HOLDS

No. 5. Being Strangled (Two Hands)

Your assailant seizes you by the throat with both hands, forcing you back against a wall, Fig. 10.

Note: In the event of being attacked in this manner, drastic methods are called for and are justifiable. We strongly recommend the application of the "Chin Jab".

1. Turn up the whites of your eyes to deceive your assailant and put him off his guard. Then suddenly shoot both your hands up inside his arms and strike him on the point of the chin—"Chin Jab".

2. Keep your fingers and thumbs extended and endeavour to reach his eyes with the points of your fingers or thumb of one of your hands. Simultaneously knee him in the pit of the stomach, Fig. 10.

DEFENCE AGAINST VARIOUS HOLDS

No. 6. "Bear Hug" (From in Front)

Your assailant, with both arms, seizes you around the body, imprisoning your arms, Fig. 11.

1. Kick him on the shins.
2. Knee him in the pit of the stomach.
3. Stamp on his feet.
4. Bump him in the face with your head.

Fig. 11

DEFENCE AGAINST VARIOUS HOLDS

No. 7. "Bear Hug" (From Behind)

Your assailant, with both arms, seizes you around the body, imprisoning your arms, Fig. 12.
1. Stamp on his feet.
2. Kick him on the shins.
3. Bump him in the face with the back of your head.

Fig. 12

DEFENCE AGAINST VARIOUS HOLDS

No. 8. Waist Hold (From in Front)

Fig. 13

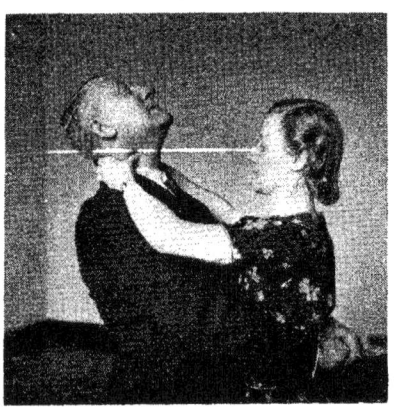

Fig. 14

DEFENCE AGAINST VARIOUS HOLDS

No. 8. Waist Hold (From in Front)

Your assailant seizes you around the body from in front, leaving your arms free.

1. Place your left hand around and in to the small of his back, simultaneously striking him on the point of the chin ("Chin Jab"). If necessary, knee him in the stomach. Fig. 13.

2. Seize his neck with both hands, fingers touching behind, thumbs in front, the points one on either side of the "Adam's Apple". Force inwards and upwards with the points of your thumbs and towards you with the points of your fingers—then jerk his head sharply backwards. Fig. 14.

Note: The average person is very susceptible to the discomfort caused by this neck hold as shown in Fig. 14, and students are advised not to practice it on their friends.

DEFENCE AGAINST VARIOUS HOLDS

No. 9. Waist Hold (From Behind)

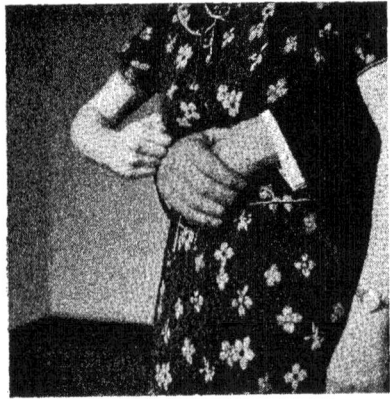

Fig. 15　　　　　　　　Fig. 15A

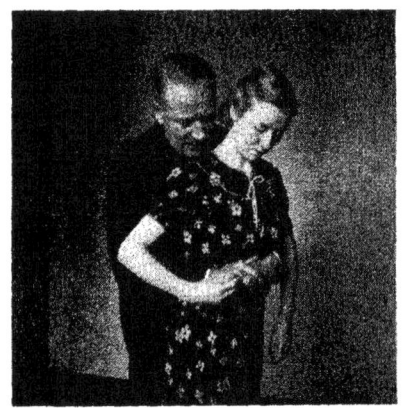
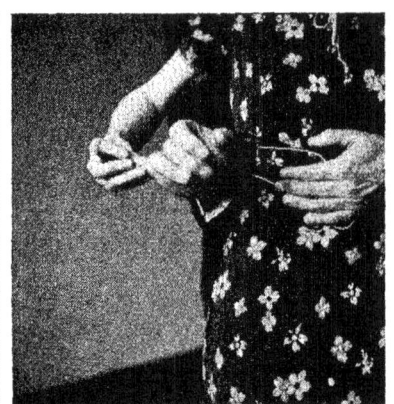

Fig. 16　　　　　　　　Fig. 16A

DEFENCE AGAINST VARIOUS HOLDS

No. 9. Waist Hold (From Behind)

Your assailant seizes you around the waist from behind, leaving your arms free.

1. Strike the back of his hand a sharp blow with your knuckles, Figs. 15 and 15A.
2. Seize either of his little fingers and bend it backwards: if necessary, break it, Figs. 16 and 16A.

Note: It should be noted that the little finger hold is the only hold on the fingers that is effective. There are many persons who could stand the pain of having one of their other fingers broken, but it is fairly safe to state not more than one person in a hundred could stand the pain of having the little finger being treated in the same way. Further, it is a sure method of making them release their hold.

3. Stamp on his feet with the heel of your shoe simultaneously striking him in the face with the back of your head.

DEFENCE AGAINST VARIOUS HOLDS

No. 10. Hair Hold (From Behind)

Fig. 17

Fig. 18

Fig. 19

DEFENCE AGAINST VARIOUS HOLDS

No. 10. Hair Hold (From Behind)

Your assailant seizes you by the hair, from behind, with his right hand.

1. Bend backwards and seize his hand from above, keeping a firm grip with your hands, force your head into his hand to prevent him letting go, Fig. 17.
2. Turn in towards your assailant; this will twist his wrist
3. Force your head up and bend his wrist inwards, away from his elbow, Fig. 18.

Note: The success of this method depends mainly upon the speed in which it is completed and the continuous upward pressure of your head against his hand, combined with the firm grip of his hand by both of yours.

If, when you are in the position shown in Fig. 18, your assailant attempts to use his left hand against you, immediately release your hold with the right hand and strike him on the point of the chin ("Chin Jab"), Fig. 19.

DEFENCE AGAINST VARIOUS HOLDS

No. 11. Coat Hold

Fig. 20

Fig. 21

Fig. 22

DEFENCE AGAINST VARIOUS HOLDS

No. 11. Coat Hold

Your assailant seizes you by the left shoulder with his right hand, Fig. 20.

1. Seize his right hand with your right hand and prevent him from releasing his hold.
2. Seize his right elbow with your left hand, your thumb to the left, Fig. 21.
3. With a circular upward and then downward motion of your left hand on the elbow, turn sharply outwards towards your right hand side by pivoting on your right foot and stepping across his front with your left leg, Fig. 22.
4. Keep a firm grip with your right hand to prevent him releasing his hold and apply a downward pressure on his elbow with your left hand.

Note: It should be noted that in Nos. 11 and 12, Coat Holds, and No. 13, Belt Hold, your assailant having caught hold of your clothing, etc., has placed himself at a great disadvantage and it is for this reason you endeavour to prevent him from releasing his hold until you have effectively dealt with him.

DEFENCE AGAINST VARIOUS HOLDS

No. 12. Coat Hold

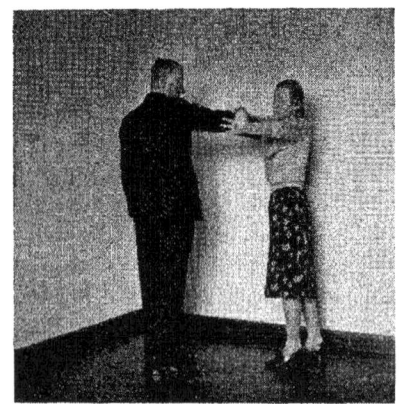

Fig. 23

Fig. 24

DEFENCE AGAINST VARIOUS HOLDS

No. 12. Coat Hold

Your assailant seizes you by the left shoulder with his right hand.

1. Seize his right elbow with your left hand from underneath; at the same time pass your right hand over the arm and seize the elbow with your right hand above your left, Fig. 23.

2. With a circular upward and downward motion of your hands on his elbow turn sharply outwards towards your right hand side. This will bring you into the position shown in Fig. 24.

3. Force his elbow towards your body and push up with your left shoulder. This will prevent him from releasing his arm. If necessary, knee him in the face with your right knee.

DEFENCE AGAINST VARIOUS HOLDS

No. 13. Belt Hold

Fig. 25

Fig. 26

DEFENCE AGAINST VARIOUS HOLDS

No. 13. Belt Hold

Your assailant seizes you by the belt with his right hand.

1. Seize his right hand from above with your right hand and prevent him from releasing his hold.
2. Seize his right elbow with your left hand from underneath, thumb to the left, Fig. 25.

Note: The success of the method depends upon the correct position of your left hand upon your assailant's right elbow and special attention must be paid to the position of your left thumb.

3. With a circular upward and then downward motion of your left hand on the elbow, turn sharply towards your right hand side by pivoting on your right foot, simultaneously stepping across his front with your left leg, Fig. 26.

Note: Providing you have prevented him from releasing his hold of your belt this will be found to be a very effective hold.

DEFENCE AGAINST VARIOUS HOLDS

No. 14. Simple Counters

Fig. 27

Fig. 27A

Fig. 28

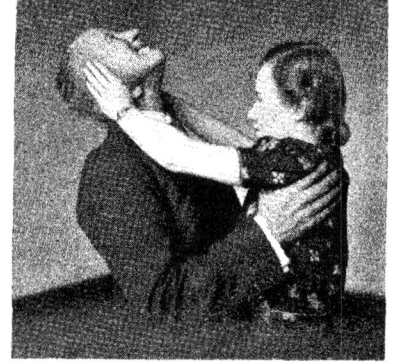

Fig. 28A

DEFENCE AGAINST VARIOUS HOLDS

No. 14. Simple Counters

(*A*) *Hand Shake*: It frequently happens that you meet a person who is very proud of his gripping powers and takes great pleasure, when shaking hands, in gripping your hand with all his strength, apparently with the idea of convincing you that he is a real "he-man", Fig. 27.

It is a very simple matter for you to take the conceit out of him—Place the *point* of your right thumb on the back of his hand between the thumb and index finger as in Fig. 27A.

Note: Only a very small amount of pressure with the point of your thumb is necessary to counteract his grip and as the intention is to take the conceit out of him, do not make it obvious by applying more pressure than is necessary.

(*B*) *Against Being Lifted.* A person attempts to lift you up by catching hold of you under the arm-pits. To prevent this: force the points of your thumbs up and into his neck close alongside the jaw bone as in Figs. 28 and 28A. Push upwards and force his head slightly backwards, which will place him off balance, making it impossible for him to lift you.

THE UMBRELLA AS A MEANS OF DEFENCE

No. 15. Umbrella Drill

A. Ready.   B. Across the Stomach.   C. Up under the Chin.

D. Down the Face.   E. Handle across Face.   F. Up under the Chin.

THE UMBRELLA AS A MEANS OF DEFENCE

No. 15. Umbrella Drill

The present day umbrella, which is around 18 to 20 inches in length, is an ideal weapon for the purpose of defence against the more serious methods of attack, and students are advised to study and make themselves thoroughly acquainted with the application of the various blows, as demonstrated:

DRILL MOVEMENTS

A = Right hand above—left hand below.
Point of umbrella to the left hand side.
B = Point, across the stomach.
C = Point up under the chin.
D = Point, down the face.
E = Handle, up across the face.
F = Up under the chin—aim to strike your opponent's "Adam's Apple" with the centre of the umbrella.

Note: In the following pages only one position of attack by an assailant has been shown. This is done so as not to confuse the student when learning. There are, of course, numerous other positions your assailant could adopt when attacking you, but providing you make yourself proficient in the use of the umbrella, at least one or two of the "Drill Strokes", perhaps with a slight variation, will more than enable you to deal effectively with any assailant.

THE UMBRELLA AS A MEANS OF DEFENCE

No. 16. Being Held from in Front

Fig. 29

Fig. 30

Fig. 31

Fig. 32

THE UMBRELLA AS A MEANS OF DEFENCE

No. 16. Being Held from in Front

CAUTION: Never attempt to strike your assailant over the head with your umbrella. The utmost injury that you could inflict with the handle of an umbrella in the event of your being successful would not be sufficient to make him release his hold, and would most likely only make him annoyed or angry with you. Further, a blow at the head, with any weapon such as a stick or umbrella, is in nine out of ten cases "telegraphed" that it is going to be given, with the result that it is a very simple matter to prevent it reaching its mark—see Fig. 29.

Having been "Held Up" as in Fig. 30, your assailant having hold of your shoulder or arms with one or both hands:

1. Hold your umbrella as in Fig. 31, right hand above, left hand below, with an interval of approximately six inches between your hands.

2. Strike your assailant with the point of the umbrella across the stomach, just below or above the belt line, by shooting your left hand forward and towards your right hand side, simultaneously pulling the umbrella backwards with your right hand. This will bring your assailant to the position shown in Fig. 32.

[continued on page 37

THE UMBRELLA AS A MEANS OF DEFENCE

No. 16. Being Held from in Front

Fig. 33

Fig. 34

Fig. 35

Fig. 36

THE UMBRELLA AS A MEANS OF DEFENCE

No. 16. Being Held from in Front

3. Should your assailant still retain his hold (which is most unlikely) strike him under the chin with the point of the umbrella by jabbing upwards with both hands as in Fig. 33.

4. In the event of missing your assailant's chin with the point of the umbrella, strike at his face by hitting downwards with your left hand, simultaneously drawing back with your right hand as in Fig. 34.

5. Continue your defence by shooting your right hand forward and towards your left hand side striking your assailant across the face in the region of the nose with the handle of the umbrella as in Fig. 35.

6. If necessary strike him under the chin as in Fig. 36.

A DEFENCE AGAINST WANDERING HANDS

No. 17. The "Cinema" Hold

Fig. 37

Fig. 38

Fig. 39

A DEFENCE AGAINST WANDERING HANDS

No. 17. The "Cinema" Hold

1. You are sitting on a chair and a hand is placed on your left knee as in Fig. 37.
2. Catch hold of the hand with your right hand, passing your fingers and thumb under the palm of the hand as in Fig. 38. Although it is rather essential that the initial hold of the offending hand should be as near as possible to that shown, you should not have any difficulty in obtaining it, as the person concerned will most likely be under the impression that you are simply returning his caress.
3. Keeping a firm grip of the hand, lift it from your knee, pulling it across your body, towards your right hand side, Fig. 39.

[*continued on page* 41

A DEFENCE AGAINST WANDERING HANDS

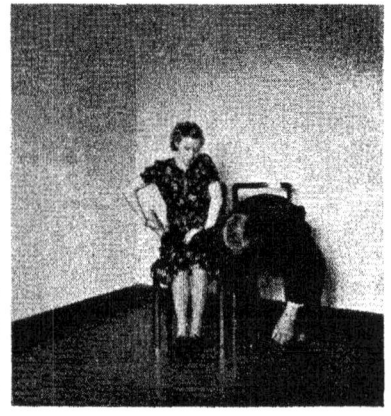

No. 17. The "Cinema" Hold

Fig. 40

Fig. 41

Fig. 42

A DEFENCE AGAINST WANDERING HANDS

No. 17. The "Cinema" Hold

4. Twist the hand and arm away from you, simultaneously seizing his elbow from above, as in Fig. 40.

5. Forcing the arm downwards, by pressing on the elbow with your left hand and twisting the arm with your right hand, until it is in the position shown in Fig. 41.

6. By keeping a reasonable pressure on the elbow and a fairly firm grip of the hand, it is impossible for your opponent to move. An alternative method of holding your opponent is to apply pressure on his elbow with your left forearm as in Fig. 42.

Note: (A) For the purpose of clearness the various movements in the "Cinema" Hold have been demonstrated sitting in ordinary chairs in the front row. Had they been demonstrated as taking place in the second or back row, the opponent's head would have been smashed on to the backs of the front seats.

(B) Students should note that after their opponent's offending hand has been secured, as demonstrated in Fig. 38, all other movements of this hold are continuous. The amount of pain or discomfort inflicted on your opponent depends upon the speed in which the various movements are completed.

(C) In the event of your opponent anticipating the application of this hold, it naturally follows that it might be difficult to apply. That being so and the circumstances justifying it—we recommend the application of one of the "Matchbox" Defences as demonstrated on pages 43 to 47.

THE MATCHBOX DEFENCE

No. 18. Matchbox (Warning)

Fig. 43

THE MATCHBOX DEFENCE

No. 18. Matchbox (Warning)

The use of the matchbox is one of the most drastic methods of defence that it is possible to employ and must only be used when the situation calls for drastic action. Further, students are warned to be extremely careful when testing the force of the blow on themselves (Fig. 43), otherwise it is quite possible for them to render themselves unconscious.

The advantage of using a matchbox, as compared with a stick or other weapon, lies in the surprise and complete unexpectedness of this form of attack. Practically four out of five persons these days carry a matchbox and any person not previously aware of this method of defence, seeing you take an ordinary matchbox out of a purse or pocket, would not be suspicious or on his guard.

There are several situations in which the use of a matchbox might easily be the only possible means of defence:

(A) You are driving a car and have picked up a hitch-hiker; he suddenly sticks a gun in your ribs. (See page 45.)

(B) You are unexpectedly stopped on a dark road with a demand "Give me a light" or "Hand over the bag". (See page 47.)

THE MATCHBOX DEFENCE

No. 19. Car "Hold-Up"

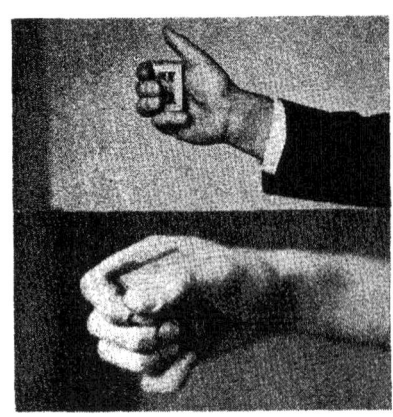

Fig. 44   Fig. 45    Fig. 46

Fig. 47    Fig. 48

THE MATCHBOX DEFENCE

No. 19. Car "Hold-Up"

You are driving a car (right-hand drive), and have picked up a hitch-hiker. He suddenly sticks a gun in your ribs.

1. Take the matchbox and hold it as in Fig. 44, the top of the box being slightly below the finger and thumb, the box resting if possible, on the little finger, Fig. 45.

2. Keeping the upper part of the right arm firmly against the right side of your body, with a circular upward motion of your right hand, pivoting your body from the hip (Fig. 46), strike your opponent on the jaw bone, anywhere between the ears and the point of the chin, Fig. 47. Simultaneously seizing the gun from above with your left hand, turning the muzzle away from your body as in Fig. 48. If you have struck your opponent correctly he will be "OUT".

Note: (A) Students must in practice check up against the fatal error committed by most of "telegraphing" their intentions, by drawing back their striking hand. The blow starts from the original position of the hand when the matchbox was first put into position. The strength or force of the blow depends mainly upon the follow-through of the body, not in the strength of the arm.

(B) In the event of your opponent being on your right hand side take the matchbox in your left hand; the blow will be equally effective.

THE MATCHBOX DEFENCE

No. 20. "Give Me a Light"

Fig. 49

Fig. 50

Fig. 51

THE MATCHBOX DEFENCE

No. 20. "Give Me a Light"

You are unexpectedly stopped on a dark road with a demand, "Give me a light" or "Hand over your bag".

The usual method of approach is for your opponent to suddenly step out of an alleyway or from behind a tree as you are about to pass, when your position would be somewhat as shown in Fig. 49.

1. Take the matchbox as in Fig. 50, the top of the box being slightly below the finger and thumb, the box resting, if possible, on the little finger.

2. It should be noted that the method of striking is somewhat different to that shown previously. In Fig. 51, your opponent being on his feet and very close to you, calls for the blow to be delivered upwards. The force of the blow depends on the follow-through, which in this case is from the right hip, leg, and foot.

Note: An alternative method—if the situation is serious enough to justify such drastic action—is: take a matchbox with the heads of the matches on top—strike a match and set fire to the matches, immediately throwing it into your assailant's face.

CONCLUSION

"Never start something that you cannot finish" is an old saying used in nearly every country throughout the world and it is with this thought in mind that we would bring this book to a conclusion.

The handbag, handkerchief, or glove, etc., are frequently mentioned in books as a method of defence, and in some they are demonstrated showing how, by a flick in the eyes, you would have your opponent at your mercy. We admit that a blow in the eye with any one of these articles could be a very painful experience for your opponent, but we know that the chances of your being successful, should you attempt to put it in practice, are very remote, and we doubt if it could be successfully accomplished once in twenty times, which definitely condemns it as a method of defence for girls.

It is admitted that the handbag, etc., as an aid to throwing your opponent off his guard, so as to enable you to secure a hold or throw, can be very effective, but it is essential that anyone employing them must be an expert in the art of defence, otherwise they would not be quick enough to see an opening if it was offered.

The average girl, as compared to a man, is handicapped far too much in weight and strength when trying to defend herself, and unless she is clever enough to spring a surprise upon her assailant and effectively deal with the situation, it is not advisable that she should "start something that cannot be finished".

We have previously mentioned that "to take the fight to your opponent's camp is seventy-five per cent of the battle won". This has been very carefully demonstrated throughout this book, which has been written for the average healthy girl so as to enable her to deal effectively with a number of what might be very unpleasant circumstances, but it is only right that we should warn her—Never Start Something You Cannot Finish.

Lightning Source UK Ltd.
Milton Keynes UK
UKOW04f1831291217
315238UK00001B/364/P